Most of us end up with
no more than five or six people
who remember us.

Teachers have thousands of
people who remember them
for the rest of their lives.

~ Andy Rooney

180 Ways to Enhance Your Success as a Teacher

Louise Paris

(and over 90 educators, parents, and students)

WALKTHETALK.COM

WALKTHETALK.COM

Resources for Personal and Professional Success

To order additional copies of this handbook, or for information
about other WALK THE TALK® products and services,
contact us at
1.888.822.9255
or visit
www.walkthetalk.com

A+ Teaching: 180 Ways to Enhance Your Success as a Teacher

Printed in the United States of America
10 9 8 7 6 5 4 3 2 1

Printed by MultiAd

$12.95
ISBN 978-1-885228-83-3
51295>

9 781885 228833

CONTENTS

ACKNOWLEDGMENTS

There are numerous people to thank for my own achievements and the production of this book:

My family and best supporters – particularly my late parents who encouraged me to become a teacher from the time I was a small child, "playing teacher." Although neither was a high school graduate, they understood and passed on the importance of education to all three of their children who became teachers with master's degrees. I am extremely grateful to my husband of 36 years, Ray, for his technology skills, being available whenever I needed him. I thank my two children, Chad and Nicole, for their endless patience, understanding, and support throughout my teaching career and during this project. And a big thank you to my sister, teacher, and school psychologist, Jean, who was always on the other end of the phone to listen to my teaching stories. You were my stress relief!

My first principal, Robert Muske, who believed in me, nudged me, and gave me the opportunities and confidence to assume leadership roles so I could realize my full potential.

The Walk The Talk Company – a welcoming group of hard-working people. Special thanks to its president, Eric Harvey, for responding to my "have you ever considered" e-mail and taking the time to build a rapport which led to his confidence in my ability to write this book. Finally, I can't thank my editor, Steve Ventura, enough for his patience, expertise, writing flair, and guidance in helping me become a first-time book author.

I thank you all!

INTRODUCTION

Congratulations!

You are unique and special. You are needed. You play a critically important role. You, along with every other member of your profession, have earned the honor and privilege of proudly proclaiming:

"I am a TEACHER!"

No one has to tell you that along with that title comes a great deal of joy, satisfaction, and personal fulfillment. That is, after all, why you do what you do. But you also know that teaching involves more than a backpack full of challenges as well. As classroom and administrative experiences become more stressfully demanding, you may be tempted to question your "career choice." Fact is, you have chosen more than a career. You have responded to a professional calling – one that places significant weight on your shoulders. Ultimately, it's your job to guide students in becoming caring, productive citizens who have acquired the intellectual and social skills to be contributing members of society.

Sound scary? Somewhat! But don't allow that responsibility to shake your confidence. Think about it this way: You are truly lucky. You're one of the fortunate people who have been blessed with a wonderful talent (and an equally wonderful opportunity) TO TEACH! So, be thankful for that talent and give the gift of yourself to the students whose lives you touch every day. Continuously strive to be the best teacher possible with the understanding that doing so takes time, patience, energy, determination, self-reflection, and commitment.

If you're like most dedicated teachers, you already are effective! You work diligently ... you do your job well. But just as it's important for your students to always try to do better, it's equally important for you. Your goal, then, is to become *even more* effective ... to be an **"A+ Teacher."**

> *You owe that to your students* – the ones who depend on you for guidance and look to you as a role model for effort and continuous improvement.
>
> *You owe that to your stakeholders* – the parents, colleagues, administrators, taxpayers, and community members who have entrusted you with the development of our greatest resources: our youth.
>
> *You owe that to yourself* – the one who enjoys the pride and satisfaction that come from making a truly positive and lasting difference in young people's lives.

So, what exactly is teacher effectiveness? **What is A+ Teaching?** Many things! There is no single definition. For some people, it may be developing and maintaining successful classroom management skills. For others, it may be enabling students to outperform state, local, and national test scores. To be sure, it will vary, depending on your district's goals and initiatives. There is, however, a myriad of teaching behaviors, practices, and attributes which are universal to a quality education – many of which you'll find on the pages that follow.

Quality teaching is demanding work! It involves developing impressive communication skills, being organized, setting daily goals, and having a willingness to make changes. It means knowing your curriculum well, being able to successfully assess learning, interpret data, and use those results to drive instruction. **A+ Teaching is even more demanding!**

A+ Teaching goes far beyond the practice of delivering curriculum and assessing learning. It's about balance – the balance between the act of teaching and the interactions of a kind-hearted human. One without the other limits any teacher's potential for greatness. Developing and showing genuine compassion, empathy, understanding, and kindness toward students will last a lot longer in their hearts and minds than a specific curricular lesson. Your kindness will demonstrate that you acknowledge and celebrate your students as physical, emotional, and intellectual beings!

A+ Teaching also involves the use of a wide range of successful ideas and activities. This means learning new strategies and trying what has worked for others. The good news: You don't have to reinvent the wheel! This handbook offers **180 practical activities, tips, and strategies** for you to apply in your daily teaching. They come from this author and a variety of teachers, parents, and students who have contributed ideas based on their own educational experiences. Hopefully, you'll be as excited to try them as I am to share them – as together we rediscover that …

- Establishing positive relationships and building a caring community is essential to student success;

- Organization of systems, materials, and the classroom environment helps your days run more smoothly;

- Communication is essential for all stakeholders to reach their common goals;

- Decisive, creative decision-making skills are crucial when the unexpected occurs;

- Incorporating brain-based strategies and responsive classroom activities significantly enhances student performance.

Whether you are a new or experienced teacher – no matter if you teach preschool, elementary, middle, or high school students – there's something here for you – and for all of your colleagues.

I'd like to share with you two recent experiences that reaffirmed for me that I, for sure, have chosen the right profession. Having just completed my thoughts of gratitude (explained later in the book), I sat down at my computer to check my e-mails. Among the many communications was a "friend" request from a professional network site that I hadn't kept up with in quite awhile. I clicked on the name and found this:

Current: *Physics teacher*

Past: *Student in Ms. Paris' class (she was the best teacher in my life).*

Post: *I'd like to add you to my professional network. You are my inspiration for teaching excellence.*

And, on another social network friend request that morning, I found:

Hi Ms. Paris. I was in your third grade class in '78-'79. You have been my inspiration for excellence in teaching throughout my 17 (yr.) career as a high school physics teacher. I would be honored if you would accept my friendship request. THANK YOU for everything and for nurturing my love of learning!

Unable to define a moment like that, I know that one of the indescribable benefits of our profession is that there are many more lives out there whose hearts and minds have been touched by us. With that in mind, use these suggestions, strategies, and activities to lead your students toward greater success. And, perhaps, because of your skill and inspiration, some of your students may someday be able to claim,

"I, too, am a TEACHER!"

Chapter 1

The Best Place for Learning

Creating a Safe and Caring Environment

It's no secret that maintaining a safe and orderly learning climate is one of the most important characteristics of successful schools – it's a fact! And while you may not realize it, you – the classroom teacher – are the single most powerful influence in creating that environment.

Although maintaining a safe school environment requires the efforts of all personnel, most of the day-to-day interactions involve you. You are the one who establishes an emotionally-safe setting ... a place where students feel free from ridicule, criticism, sarcasm, inferiority, and failure. You accomplish this through consistent guidance and by showing genuine compassion and empathy for every student. Classroom management struggles tend to minimize once you create a safe learning environment in which your students feel respected, cared for, and encouraged.

Emotional security is one of the main ingredients in each student's recipe for academic success!

Creating a safe, orderly environment begins by building rapport with your students on the first day of school. You'll need to establish trusting relationships with each student as well as encourage the students to form trusting relationships with each other.

Additionally, building an emotionally safe environment involves setting guidelines, modeling expected behavior, and teaching problem-solving skills and strategies, social competence, and character education so that a productive, caring community emerges.

Here's something to always remember: A positive environment starts with you and the image you project. When you show that you like what you are doing and are happy to be there – and that you care about every child and plan to do your best to help them all – your students will look forward to coming to school each day. Young people depend so much on what you do and how you do it. They take their cues from you. For the most part, you are their powerhouse ... you are the guardian of the safe haven they need to succeed! The ideas that follow are intended to help you meet that all-important responsibility.

Recognizing that you probably do many of these activities at the start of each new school year already, they are intentionally included to show the gradual development of a safe and caring learning community. Do not be put off by their simplicity. These are good reminders ... proven ways to help make your environment the best place for learning!

1. **Provide a warm, welcoming classroom.** Hand out name tags for the students (and you) to wear on the first few days of school. Stand at the classroom door every day to greet each student by name, with a smile and a friendly comment such as, "Good morning. I'm so happy to see you this morning," or "Welcome back. We missed you while you were absent." Make sure every student's name is included on bulletin boards, activity lists, helper charts, and other places to show that *everyone* is an important part of your classroom community.

2. **Create a sense of belonging for new students.** Coming into a new school or even a new class can be a tough challenge for the "new kid." Have students organize an all-school welcoming committee in which they plan an orientation, school tours, social events, and meetings to help incoming families transition into their new community. Consider assigning a "student concierge" – one of your more responsible students to be the new kid's new friend. It may not lead to a lasting friendship, but it will surely give the new student a more comfortable assimilation into his or her unfamiliar class while giving your "concierge" a shot of confidence and some practical human relation skills. Everybody wins!

3. **Create opportunities for you and your students to get well acquainted**. Before the start of the new school year, send each student a "Welcome to My Class" note. Include a brief introduction and bio of yourself. Then, on the first day of school, have students complete a "Getting to Know You" inventory that includes favorites, pet peeves, interests, talents, hobbies, etc. Ask students to share their information with the entire class, then collect the sheets and file them for future use. **Use them as references** for parent/teacher conferences. A specific comment about a child could be a very impressive opener to a parent meeting: "You must be very proud of your child's musical talent. I understand that Rebecca plays the piano quite well."

4. **Help students get better acquainted with each other.** Do some icebreaker activities throughout the first few days of school. For example, make and distribute table tents with conversation starters such as, *What is your favorite book? How many siblings do you have? Do you have any pets? If so, describe them.* Have students interview each other in pairs and then introduce their partners and present their answers to the class.

5. **Build rapport with your students.** Continuous interactions with each student – lighthearted chats, sharing common interests, complimenting each other, exchanging photographs of family and pets, etc. – are magical rapport-building moments. Personalize your student/teacher relationships by planning a luncheon "date" with each student as a way to continue those noncurriculum-related conversations. Then, about one month into the school year, send a handwritten letter to each individual in your class. Include the successes and positive qualities of that student along with encouragement to persevere and stay on the path of kindness, responsibility, and consistent improvement.

6. **Build trusting relationships with your students** by extending yourself beyond the classroom dynamic. Our relationships with students must go beyond reading, writing, and math if we want to build a community that promotes excellence. Get to know your students even better by meeting individually and asking about their hopes, dreams, goals, and fears.

   In addition to making those personal connections, keeping your word with students is one of the very best ways to build trust. Whether you keep your word by following through with rewards, implementing consequences when necessary, or by saying what you mean and meaning what you say, students will rise to any challenge because they trust you!

> *To be trusted is a greater compliment*
> *than to be loved.*
> ~ George MacDonald

7. **Foster a community environment.** Conduct a class meeting at the beginning of each day. During this time, students sit inform-ally in a circle on the floor or on chairs. Activities include greeting each other, discussing current events, sharing "upnews" (upbeat news) of the day, problem solving, group decision-making, brief fun games, social skills discussions, and other communication and community-building activities.

8. **Teach and model desired social skills.** In addition to teaching academics, we are charged with helping children develop the social skills necessary to be successful in life – like getting along with others. Teaching and encouraging your students to practice good manners will help improve their social interactions. Being courteous and polite, extending greetings, and verbalizing sincere apologies are all important life skills.

Teach your students how to use the "Perfect Apology" in which the offender explains *what* he or she is sorry for and *how* they plan to mend the relationship.

Be sure to *model* friendliness and politeness. For example, as you walk through the building with your class, address adults with a "Good morning, Mr./Mrs. _____." Be obvious about issuing compliments. The things we do and say determine how people view us. Good manners contribute toward positive impressions. Not all students will be math wiz kids, but all students CAN learn simple manners!

9. **Keep your eyes and ears open.** Listen to and observe social interactions between students – both inside and outside of the classroom. Are they able to control their feelings and impulses? Do they respect themselves and others? Do they work well alone and with a group? Through your observations you will know when to intervene and which skills to teach them: problem solving, communication, interpreting social cues, etc. Follow up with a "social conference" to discuss behavioral boundaries and accept-able alternatives. Involve students in solving their problems.

10. **Maintain your cool!** Act or react calmly during those frustrating moments that everyone has from time to time. Even though you may want to scream or cry, count to ten. Be patient. Try this strategy as a reminder to stay grounded: Ask students to select a code word that someone in the class can say when they notice your edges starting to fray. If anyone begins to feel your tension, they can say that word out loud as a cue for you to take a deep breath and compose yourself. It is important for students to see real-life demonstrations of adults handling anger, frustration, and disappointment appropriately.

11. **Acknowledge and be sensitive to student feelings.** Children's feelings are very real and should never be dismissed as trivial or insignificant. As a teacher, you have a responsibility to notice and address student feelings of loneliness, sadness, anxiety, anger, fear, confusion, or depression. Casual, private one-on-one time is a valuable way to explore what you notice. Deliver your words carefully in a positive and supportive manner. Avoid scolding. Reprimand cautiously. Preface your comments with a positive statement like: "You know I like you, but I wouldn't be a good teacher if I didn't help you become the best you can be – and right now I don't think that's happening."

12. **Teach students to affirm themselves and each other.** Have them practice positive statements such as …

I can solve my own problems!
I am a good and worthwhile person!
I can do this!
I can move past my mistakes!

13. **Observe, acknowledge, and praise positive attitudes and behaviors** and you will encourage more of the same. You might want to casually mention your observations by saying, "I noticed how friendly you were when you entered the building today. I feel good when people say hi to me, don't you?" Remember that reinforced behaviors tend to be repeated behaviors.

14. **Facilitate and encourage positive peer relationships.** Create occasional grouping opportunities throughout the day. Pairings such as reading buddies, peer tutors, and playground pals help students develop friendships. Mix up seating arrangements from time to time. Regroup working clusters so that students will interact with different classmates. Once a week, offer the option of having each student journal to another classmate – requiring the receiver to journal back as a courtesy.

15. **Model and teach appreciation.** At the end of each day, thank your class for one thing that they did during the day. Write your gratitude thought on the board. It might say, "Thank you for an enjoyable and productive math lesson today." Be as specific as possible. Give students a few minutes to write in their gratitude journals (notebooks designated only for expressions of gratitude) about one thing that happened that day that they are thankful for. Fostering gratitude encourages students to be thankful for what they have. It is a way to embrace the life they're in – appreciating the little things we all so often take for granted.

16. **Plan goals with each student – set high expectations.**
Schedule a goal setting session with each student. Evaluate
past goals and discuss successes – no matter how small they
may be. After reviewing progress and building confidence, work
on setting more advanced goals – assuring the student that you
will be there to help. Use goal setting for social as well as academic skills. For example: On cards, brightly colored papers, or
foam sheets with a magnet on the back, write a one-word soft
skill on each (*cooperative, kind, hard-working,* etc.). At the start
of every week, pick one soft skill and have each student write a
goal to help him/her improve that particular skill.

17. **Develop behavioral guidelines.** With input from your students,
establish your classroom guidelines. Students are more likely to
respect the rules when they are included in defining them. Keep
them simple, brief, and behavioral. For example, *Respect all
others as well as ourselves ... Respect our environment and
everything in it.* Discuss the expectations. Be specific. Students
cannot monitor their own behavior unless they know exactly what
it is they should be doing.

18. **Establish and enforce consequences for inappropriate
behavior.** Make consequences clear. For example, "If you use
inappropriate language, this is the consequence: View two parent-
approved prime-time TV shows tonight and copy any phrases
or comments that contain inappropriate language. Next to those
comments, write a more appropriate way of saying that sentence."
The consequence is related to the offense and requires the
student to think in more acceptable ways. Enforce consequences
that are relevant and offer learning opportunities. Discuss what
the student did and why it is unacceptable. Be consistent in your
enforcement, and make sure that parents are informed.

19. **Use a positive approach to discipline.** Your approach to discipline impacts attitudes, learning, and school safety. Avoid confrontations whenever possible. Make consequences meaningful and appropriate to the offense. Create win-win situations by offering choices ("Would you rather finish your work during your recess or at home tonight?"). Instead of criticism, ask students, "What was good about what you did?" … "What wasn't good about what you did?"… "What would you do differently if you could do it over?" Listen and conclude with the question, "How can I help you?"

20. **Be an eclectic disciplinarian.** Just as there are no two students alike, there is no single foolproof method of discipline. Become familiar with many positive approaches to discipline. Do some library and Internet research. Ask your colleagues about their experiences. If one approach doesn't work, try another, since all students respond differently. Just make sure that your actions are equitable in terms of severity and appropriateness.

21. **Embrace your role as a mediator!** When there is a conflict between two or more students, step in and take action. Work with the involved parties to help them resolve their issues. Bring them together. Make sure they respectfully speak to each other (rather than to you). Do your best to remain neutral and nonjudgmental.

Additionally …

22. **Don't play the "blame game."** When intervening in conflict situations, avoid questions like, "Who started this?" or "Who's at fault here?" Such inquiries tend to produce defensiveness and increase tension. Keep everyone focused on finding solutions rather than pointing fingers.

23. **Teach students conflict resolution strategies.** Here's one you might want to try:

"The Peace Connection"

Facing each other, two disputants alternately recite
and verbally fill in the blanks of each step.

Step 1: "I'm feeling _____ right now because _____."

Step 2: "Because I want to understand what went wrong,
please tell me the reason for _____."

Step 3: *Response to request in step #2.*

Step 4: "So what I hear you saying is _____."

Step 5: "I'm thinking that we could have handled this differently
by _____."

Step 6: "This is what I want from you _____."

Step 7: "I'll try to give you what you need or want by _____."

Step 8: "I'm willing to try this plan and revisit it in a week."

Step 9: "Thank you."

24. **Respect their personal space.** If a student pulls away when you try to put your hand on his or her shoulder (or similar well-intended gestures), be assured that there is a reason for the discomfort. Back off and look for alternative ways to demonstrate warmth and caring. Change your approach with that student – paying close attention to any gestures that seem to be well received.

25. **Make the most of mistakes.** If you make a mistake, own up to it, apologize, and fix it as best as you can. Students will respect you for your honesty. Downplay student mistakes. Saying something like, "We're all here to learn" is just one comment that might make a pupil feel more comfortable with a wrong response. Help everyone understand through discussions that it is okay to make an occasional mistake and to fail, and that failure can be a key stepping stone to success. Point to the many stories of inventors and creators who failed repeatedly (like Thomas Edison) on the way to extraordinary successful achievements. Keep the focus on learning from the error and trying not to repeat it.

Mistakes o▪r are learning opportunities in disguise!

26. **Teach students how to deal with disappointment.** Start with grades. Have private discussions with students who have not achieved their anticipated or desired grade on assignments. Ask them to share their feelings and remind them that there will be future opportunities to improve. Express confidence in them and emphasize the importance of setting realistic goals. Remind them that few people can get A's all the time, but everyone can work hard and give their very best effort.

27. **Infuse character education into your day.** Model and reinforce important "core values" such as empathy, honesty, responsibility, thoughtfulness, respect, consideration, kindness, cooperation, and compassion. Comments from you such as, "I respect and admire people who are honest" or "That was very thoughtful of you" help to reinforce desired traits and behaviors.

28. Incorporate character education into your curriculum. One way to do that is through the stories that you read aloud. Ask reflective discussion questions such as, "Do you feel that this character could have made a better choice? Why or why not? What would you have done in that situation?" Another way to teach responsibility, respect, and compassion is to invite some-one from the local Humane Society to demonstrate proper pet care. Hopefully, students will begin to transfer their compassion for animals toward humans as well.

29. Educate on expectations. Rather than just communicating your expectations, teach them! Don't expect students to know how to "do" school. For example, how do you expect students to come into your classroom? Teach what you expect, then practice the right ways. From greetings to group work, you and your students will be more effective if you teach, practice, and revisit.

30. Watch out for bullying. Be a bully-buster! Stay on the alert for sarcastic, rude comments in the classroom and other areas of the school. Pay attention if students are reluctant to leave your room during recess breaks. Confront bullying. If you see it, hear it, or hear about it, investigate. Stop it, get help, give guidance, report, and document it. Be familiar with, and follow, any related district policies.

31. Teach tolerance. It is critical that students respect each other's differences in order to avoid conflicts that often result from a lack of understanding. One way to recognize and embrace differences is by acknowledging and celebrating ethnic customs, traditions, and events so you can make your topics relevant to all. Teach inclusion through example. Involve everyone in activities – even though some limitations may exist. Emphasize the importance of being patient … it breeds tolerance.

32. **Model kindness and compassion.** Be kind, yourself. If you show kindness to your students, they will be more likely to show it back to you ... and to each other. It's the one language we can all understand. At the end of each school day ask yourself:

> *What did I do today to set an example*
> *for being kind and compassionate?*

33. **Launch a Kindness Campaign!** Here are a few ideas to get you started ...

Use the news. If students hear or read about a fire, flood, tornado or other misfortune, you might ask, "Is there anything we can do to help?" Solicit their suggestions and encourage them to become involved in helping. One simple, yet meaningful gesture would be sending a card to a soldier overseas – or to someone who is sick or injured, or has experienced a personal tragedy.

Create a kindness bulletin board on which students post newspaper and magazine articles that describe any kind act. Discuss each incident or situation described in the article.

Make an "acts of kindness quilt" to hang in the classroom. Whenever students do something kind for someone else, they write it on a quilt square and explain it to the class. Have the entire class applaud each time a new square is added.

Immerse the environment in positive messages such as:

> *Kindness is the Key to Happiness!*
> *Be Cool! Be Kind!*
> *Kind People are Good People!*

34. Practice "academic empathy." Walk a mile in their shoes! Reflect back to the time when you were a student. Can you remember the anxieties and frustrations of interacting with peers and teachers? Think about the times when you didn't understand something being taught. How did you feel? Keep placing yourself in your students' situation during instruction. Ask yourself, *If I were them, would I get this? How can I improve the level of understanding? How can I relate it to something in their lives?*

35. Teach students to care about their lives and everyone in it. Start by encouraging them to care about their own health – both physical and emotional. Discuss good health habits ... ways to keep the body and mind fit. Then focus on their relationships with others – family, friends, and fellow students. Modeling and requiring respect for people and property are ways you can help your kids develop caring attitudes.

36. Eat, sleep, and breathe EMOTIONAL SAFETY! Be sure to maintain discipline. Acknowledge and praise successes. Smile. Require respect at all times. Care for and accept students unconditionally. Reassure them that the classroom is a safe haven – a place where they can be themselves ... a place where it's okay to make mistakes, to misunderstand, to stumble along the way because you have their backs.

37. Keep it PHYSICALLY SAFE! As a teacher, you are responsible for the well-being of all of the students under your care. To fully meet that responsibility, you must ensure their *physical* as well as emotional safety. So, make sure your classroom meets all district, state, and federal safety requirements. Closely monitor and control any lessons that involve physical activity – including the use of sharp objects like scissors and pins. Carefully manage field trips and recess play. Guard them. Protect them. Keep them safe!

Chapter 2

Where Did I Put
That Report?

*Getting Organized to Make Your Days Function
More Smoothly*

Have you ever heard the phrase, "Don't mess with my mess"? I sure have! I've not only heard it, I've either said it or thought it more than once during my career! Those of us who are not naturally well organized often profess that – despite being surrounded by our piles of stuff – we know exactly where everything is. Unfortunately, our messes can eventually eat us alive! Sooner or later we temporarily lose something important – causing us to spend countless minutes frantically searching for the one item that was just there two days ago! We fret, we stress, and we waste our all-too-precious time. Sound familiar?

Over the years, I've learned that staying organized is essential to the flow of the school day. The organization of ideas, teacher and student materials, the classroom environment, curriculum-related and/or extra-curricular events, etc., increases the efficiency of teaching and learning.

Fact is, to be at the top of our game, we need to find ways to become super-organized. From color coding and storage bins, to checklists and idea organizers, there is a myriad of systematic approaches you can adopt to make your teaching days (and your classroom) even more efficient, productive, and enjoyable. We'll review some of them – along with many other "getting organized" ideas – on the pages that follow.

38. **Organize your classroom to accommodate everyone's needs.** For example, you might need to provide pathways and tables that allow room for a wheelchair. To accommodate students with eyesight problems, you may have to alter the size of printed materials or arrange seating in the front of the room. No matter what the special need is – physical or behavioral – provide the best environment possible to enable all students to experience comfort and success.

39. **Make sure your classroom is user-friendly.** Look around the room. Are reference charts hung too high or too low? Is everything clearly labeled? Is the print on posters and captions large enough? Do chairs and desks fit the sizes of the students? The best way to check these things is to "switch seats." Sit in several student desks and ask yourself, *If I were this student, would I be able to perform at my highest level in this location?*

40. **Check for distractions.** Highly decorated classrooms can be overwhelming and often overstimulating for some students. Are there things hanging over their heads such as artistic mobiles, posters, kites, and other decorations? Are colors calming or are they likely to evoke other emotions? Is there just too much stuff in a crowded area? These are just a few things to consider when it comes to organizing your learning space.

41. **Organize for safety.** Make sure there are safe places to keep students' materials and possessions. Do not allow students to pile things on the floor. Hanging clothing from chairs can also be a safety hazard. Instead, provide bins, cubbies, and portable cabinets for student materials. You might ask a parent to sew chair covers that contain a large pocket on the back of the chair, which can be used for notebooks or other lightweight items.

42. **Set up an index file box for student information.** This file should contain one or more index cards for each student – alphabetically arranged. Transfer key pieces of information from the "Getting to Know You" inventory (see #3). Include important health information and any accommodation requests from parents.

43. **Don't leave home without your sticky notes!** Use them to make notes about your students throughout the day. These comments can be useful when you're trying to think about something new to say on report cards or during parent conferences. At the end of the day, stick these notes onto the student's index card in your file box (see #42). They will be good references for future meetings and reports.

44. **Protect confidentiality.** Designate and maintain a secure place for student information, parent notes, report cards, test scores, health records, and all other confidential material. Do not keep them in plain view for students, parents, or others to read without your approval.

45. **Help students organize and plan their learning.** One way to do this is by teaching them to use a "**KWLU** Graphic Organizer." Provide preprinted sheets for students to complete and discuss. Each sheet has four vertical columns with the following headings:

K	W	L	U
What do I Know?	What do I Want to learn?	What did I Learn?	How will I Use this?

46. **Devise a check-in system for all assignments.** Set up a stacking bin/basket for each subject area. Inside of each basket, place a folder – with a class roster attached to the cover – for each assignment. When students turn in their work, check off their names on the roster sheet and place the completed assignment in the folder. This makes it easy to see whose work remains due – and it reduces the need for additional sorting.

47. **Store bulletin board materials by theme, caption, or subject.** Oversized artist portfolios make great storage containers for your larger board displays (pictures, posters, signs, artifacts, etc.). Labeled portfolios can be kept in your classroom, school storage area, or at home. Create a master list of their contents so you'll know exactly where to find the specific material you need.

48. **Sort your desktop at the end of each day.** File loose papers. Put pens, paper clips and other small items in the drawer. Place other non-immediately needed materials on a nearby labeled shelf. Keep your lesson plans open and easy to access. Keep the next day's activity materials visible and ready to use.

49. **Use and maintain a consistent filing system**. Decide the most useful way to arrange your teacher files: by theme, topic, subject, time of year, lesson number (matching your lesson plan), etc. In addition, you will need a filing system for teaching-related information such as articles and guidelines related to ADHD, autism, behavioral disorders, etc. Keep active files organized, updated, and within reach. Vertical file organizers are perfect for that use.

50. **Be prepared to teach each day.** Check your e-mails for last-minute messages. Review your lesson plans. Have all materials available. Visualize your day. Develop a "getting ready ritual" and follow it every morning.

51. **Keep your manuals together.** If you are an early childhood educator who teaches many subjects, you probably have piles of teacher manuals and resource books! Those should be close to your desk (easy for a substitute to locate) and placed on a shelf, labeled by subject.

52. **Never run out of pencils!** At the beginning of the school year, ask parents to donate a package of 10 pencils for a "community pencil basket." (You may want to donate them for any parents who may be financially unable.) Keep a class roster in the pencil basket. Whenever you issue a pencil, make a tally mark next to the student's name – until he/she uses up all ten of their donated pencils. This ends the all-too-common "borrowing someone else's pencil" dilemma!

53. **Use the numbering system.** In the beginning of the school year, assign students sequential numbers (starting with #1) as you go through your class list alphabetically. Each student keeps that number all year. Instead of writing names inside of their textbooks, have students use their numbers. Collect by number. When checking attendance or collecting materials, go by the numbers. It's much faster and easier to administer. And, when accounting for all students on a field trip, call out each number. A missing number means a missing child!

54. **Provide student mailboxes** – for school bulletins, newsletters, announcements, etc. Partitioned shoe organizers work great for student mailboxes. Label each mailbox with the student's name and number. Stress the importance of privacy – allowing only the owner to remove things from mailboxes without permission. Make certain students empty them at the end of each day and take the contents home.

55. **Set up a "good ideas" file.** Purchase a 3x5 file box and fill it with index cards and labeled subject dividers. Each time you think of, see, or hear about a good teaching idea, jot it down and file it for future use. Review this file often.

> *Organizing is what you do before you do something,*
> *so that when you do it, it's not all mixed up.*
>
> ~ A. A. Milne

56. **Expect the unexpected.** Do you have an organized system for field trips? Are you prepared for emergencies? Take along a class list with parent contact phone numbers, chaperone guidelines, your driver's license, cash or a credit card, a cell phone, and a belt bag with first aid items.

57. **Use an organized and efficient system for student grades.** Whenever practical, use technology for grading, test analysis, and record keeping. There are many automated grading programs available in the marketplace. If you don't have access to them, create your own record system using rubrics and traditional grading procedures. Do not let correcting and grading pile up – they are time sensitive. The sooner students know their mistakes and correct them, the faster they can learn the concept or skill.

58. **Be prepared for parent/teacher conferences.** Post your conference schedule outside of the room where you and parents will be meeting. Set up chairs and group collections of work in case the parents have to wait a few minutes. (This might be a book of student-authored stories or poems.) On a table near your conference area, arrange each collection of student items you plan to share: work samples, tests, and the report card that you will be discussing. Place the material in the scheduled order.

59. **Special events need special planning.** Do you and your class sponsor special events such as science fairs, parent breakfasts, music or drama performances, grandparent luncheons, or other family activities? If so, solicit parent volunteers to help organize the details. Form committees and meet with them to discuss your specific needs/wants. Delegate as much as possible. Send out guest invitations a month ahead of the event so they can put it on their calendars. Keep notes and written plans on file for possible use the next time similar events roll around.

60. **Teach students how to organize their desks and lockers.** Students tend to cram books and papers into their desks and lockers – making it difficult, if not impossible, to find anything in a hurry. Show them how to arrange materials by size, subject, color, etc. Require some type of zipper case for loose items. Give them sufficient time to transition from class to class. Make periodic inspections and praise those who are maintaining order.

61. **Organize your students' day by sharing your plans.** Provide a "morning message" and a schedule of the day's activities for students to read as they enter the classroom. This can be written on the board or a chart, projected on a screen, or distributed on paper. Review each day's agenda and allow for questions.

62. **Plan your work.** Make a list of that day's tasks – numbered by order of importance. Work on the highest priority items first. If you know that you have a meeting to prepare for, do that before correcting papers. At the end of the day, highlight all unfinished items. Carry those items over to the next day's list. Be sure you have completed your urgent items by the time they are needed.

63. **Work your plans.** Follow your time allocations for each subject. Stick to your lesson plans or you'll be less likely to complete everything that day. If you have planned one hour for math, try not to go beyond that time, or everything else will shift (and suffer).

64. **Be prepared for *your* goal-setting and evaluation meetings.** Simplify your goals. Select meaningful, measurable targets that connect with and support overall school and district goals. Keep records of your activities and results achieved throughout the year – and store them in a designated portfolio or computer file. If your records are computerized, print them out and have them available for each meeting.

65. **Be ready for parent concern meetings.** Avoid a train wreck! Never enter a parent concern meeting unprepared. Ask the parents to specify their concern ahead of time. Bring your notes, work samples, grades, and any other supportive evidence that relate to the issues. Limit the time to twenty or thirty minutes by scheduling the conference in front of another obligation. Be sure to find out what the parents are expecting from you and present a plan that will address their concern. Conclude by offering future help as needed. Excuse yourself and leave to avoid a lengthy, drawn-out, counterproductive situation.

66. **Make the substitute teacher's day easier.** Have a visible sub folder that contains a class roster, activity schedule, emergency drills, and all other important information. Prepare all teaching materials that he or she will need. Have specific lesson plans in an easy-to-locate place. In the event of an unexpected absence, provide generic lesson plans for each subject area. Give the name and location of a colleague who would be willing to assist your sub if necessary.

Chapter 3

Do You Hear What I Hear?

Mastering the Essentials of Communication

A successful school is like a Super Bowl-winning football team. The players depend upon each other to do their designated jobs. If the linemen don't protect their quarterback, he will be sacked … if the defensive backs don't stop passes, the other team scores. In order to do their jobs effectively, everyone must communicate with each other. It's essential for all levels of the game. The coach communicates the play to the quarterback (or defensive captain) who, in turn, passes that information along to the players. When communication is lacking, plays and game plans fall apart!

There exists a similar interdependence within the educational setting. A school's communicative interdependence is as important to its success and efficiency as an entire team's communication is to winning a football championship. Administrators and teachers determine school and teacher goals. Teachers communicate those goals to students and parents by defining the students' related goals. With the support of teachers and parents, students carry out the tasks needed to achieve their goals. When the communication is unclear, students often pursue their own agendas – missing the common goals altogether.

Students and parents depend on teachers and administrators for clear communication. Teachers and administrators depend upon each other for the very same thing. All require an efficient flow of information. Without it, established goals are difficult (at best) to meet.

One vital component of a school's success is the home/school connection. Parents can be invaluable in exploring options for change in a child's scholastic performance – as long as requests, suggestions, and goals are discussed between the teacher(s) and the parent(s). The clearer the expectations, the greater the likelihood of parental involvement. The way you, as a teacher, help bridge that understanding is through consistent, effective communication. Effective home/school communication is a win-win activity that can help everyone realize the ultimate benefit of better student performance.

Equally important is the ongoing communication between the teacher and students. Effective teacher/student communication leads to trusting relationships. It inspires, builds confidence, and motivates students to reach high expectations. That communication must be clear, specific, encouraging, positive, and meaningful.

Effective communication is not only important to you as a teacher, but for students as well. It is needed to accurately express thoughts and feelings, to interpret and pass on others' messages, to avoid conflict, to have meaningful conversations, and to engage in higher-level thinking.

> *Communication – the human connection – is the key to personal and career success.*
> ~ Paul J. Meyer

Whether playing football or working within the structure of a school, you're looking to score points … to achieve your goals. You're hoping to score touchdowns! On the following pages you'll find a collection of tips that will help you score those Super Bowl points in communication!

67. **Stop, Look, and Listen.** When a student or adult speaks to you, stop everything, make eye contact, and listen intently. Focus on their words and any messages hidden within those words. By giving your undivided attention, you ensure understanding, build trust within the relationship, and encourage the other person to approach you with future concerns.

Go beyond listening – respond!

68. *Acknowledge* **what you hear.** One way to do this is by stating, "What you're saying is…" If a student is expressing a thought in class, give a response instead of just nodding and moving on to the next person. Another acknowledgment might sound something like this, "That's an interesting way to look at it. I've never thought about it that way. Thank you for your ideas." Comments like that help the students feel accepted and valued.

69. *Act* **on what you hear.** When students are seeking resolution to a concern, assist them in the problem-solving process. They are depending on you for help. Together, plan a solution. Every concern is important – no matter how insignificant it may seem to you. If students see that you listen but do nothing about their issues, they'll stop asking for your help. Worse yet, they'll stop believing that you care.

70. **Disagree respectfully.** Consider what *you* would want to hear and *how* you would want to hear it. You can respectfully disagree with others by saying something like, "I appreciate your insightfulness, but I think we see things differently. Can I count on you to listen to my viewpoint just as I have listened to yours?"

71. **Eliminate sarcasm toward others.** Sarcasm rarely feels warm and fuzzy. A comment such as, "Duh!" can make others feel bad even though it was intended to prompt laughter.

72. **Make requests rather than issuing commands.** A student is more likely to comply when you whisper into his/her ear, "Would you help me by putting away that game?" instead of barking, "Get that game off of your desk!" Because we're human, the temptation to slip into the latter mode is always there.

73. **Give specific feedback as often as possible.** Use verbal comments or notes to share your observations. Give feedback that supports, informs, and inspires the learner. Be specific. Make sure your comments describe **the situation**, **the behavior**, and **the result**. For example, "I noticed that you really focused on detail to turn in a quality science project. Keep up the fine work!" Students respond well to positive, justifiable, sincere feedback.

74. **Fight the temptation of destructive criticism.** Avoid comments like, "You really have a bad attitude today!" or "This assignment shows no effort at all!" Instead you might ask, "Did you give this assignment your best effort?" (Self-reflection is a powerful tool.) Exercise your authority wisely. Remember that your words have a huge impact on students' confidence and feelings of self-worth.

75. **Keep projecting a positive image.** Continue to look professional, act professional, be professional! The image you project is a form of communication – about you. Are you upbeat and enthusiastic about teaching? Is your attitude positive? Are you friendly and pleasant? Do your students perceive you as approachable? Not sure? Ask them!

76. **Share your feelings with your students** so they don't take an occasional mood swing personally. Kids need to know that when teachers have a bad day, it doesn't mean that they don't like their job or their students. You may want to start an emotionally difficult day by saying, "Wow! I'm really frazzled right now, and it has nothing to do with you." Or "I'm feeling a little overwhelmed, and I'm wondering if you would help me out by working on your journals while I take a few minutes to regroup." Be sure to thank them.

77. **Teach students how to read body language.** Demonstrate and invite students to model a variety of facial expressions and gestures. Discuss the intended meaning and appropriate ways to respond.

VERBAL COMMUNICATION

Words convey **7%** of our message
Tone of voice conveys **38%** of our message
Body language conveys **55%** of our message

78. **Communicate clear expectations.** Share the objectives at the beginning of each lesson. Let students know what is expected and what they need to learn. If you are expecting quality work, students need to know what that looks like. Show a visual sample and clearly describe the expected outcome.

79. **Vary your method of providing directions.** Some students have difficulty processing verbal directions. Instead of repeating the directions for better understanding, explain your message in a different way. Use stories, examples, drawings, diagrams, charts, graphs, pictures, demonstrations, etc. Make sure written directions are specific and use understandable vocabulary.

80. **Check for understanding.** Solicit questions to determine what students understand and what may need further explanation. For example, you might say, "Tanya, if you had to ask one question, what would it be?" If you sense a lack of understanding by most of the class, ask a volunteer to help explain or demonstrate the concept in question.

81. **Be consciously aware of your nonverbal communication.** Does it facilitate or inhibit learning? Are your facial gestures friendly; are you frowning or smiling? Are your arms folded in an intimidating manner? Ask your students. Ask your colleagues. Video some of your sessions and see for yourself.

In order to create a positive, productive learning community, you need to communicate effectively – and you need to help all of your students communicate effectively, as well. Here are some ideas for doing that …

82. **Help students articulate and communicate clearly.** Teach them to verbalize complete thoughts – applying appropriate voice inflections. (For example, their voice should drop at the end of a declarative sentence.) Students should avoid using incomplete phrases. Do not accept texting shortcuts for writing assignments. Speaking and hearing correct language help transfer it correctly to their written communication.

83. **Insist that students speak kindly to others.** Use the *rewind strategy*. If you hear a student lash out at another, say, "Stop! Rewind!" (You could also use "instant replay.") This is a cue for the student to stop and think about what was said and how it was delivered. It's his or her "do over" opportunity. The next step is for the student to restate it in a kinder way.

84. **Teach students to encourage and support each other.** Solicit and list supportive comments that are genuine and justifiable – not superficial compliments. Post the list in the classroom and refer to it often. Provide opportunities during group activities for students to encourage and support each other. You might ask, "How did you feel about _____'s contributions? Did you tell her how interesting her ideas were?"

85. **Teach how to paraphrase for understanding.** Try grouping students in pairs. Each pair selects an agreed-upon book. One student is the reader; the other is the paraphraser. The reader reads several sentences from a character's dialog. Then, the paraphraser retells that character's message in his or her own words. Both discuss whether the message was the same as the original source. Finally, switch roles and repeat the process so that each has the opportunity to paraphrase.

Along that same line …

86. **Teach students the skill of active listening.** Use role-playing activities to demonstrate and develop this skill. Students should practice listening – distraction-free – with eye contact and total attention to the speaker's message. Work with everyone to over-come the common trap of formulating a response before the other person has finished speaking.

> *We all have been taught how to speak, how to read, and how to write. But few of us have actually ever been TAUGHT how to listen.*
> ~ Eric Harvey

87. **Brainstorm ways to respectfully disagree.** One example might be, "I respect your opinion even though I have different thoughts about that." Solicit and list similar comments on a chart and post them in the classroom. Provide opportunities to practice them.

88. **Teach students to respect others' opinions.** Make it clear that laughing at someone's thoughts, ideas, or opinions is never acceptable! That behavior needs some consequence or it will be contagious. Have your class help determine the consequence. Encourage students to make positive comments such as, "I like that idea!" or "That's great thinking on your part!"

89. **Encourage thinking out loud.** For example, when soliciting an answer to a problem, ask probing questions that will encourage students to explain their thinking. In math, it might sound like this: "Since I know that twenty plus twenty equals forty, I just took forty and subtracted one to get the answer for twenty plus nineteen."

90. **Ask questions that encourage higher-level thinking.** Ask many open-ended questions. Go deeper with your questioning. For example, "What are your thoughts about … Describe what you would have done … What do you think would have happened if …? Allow time for students to formulate their answers.

91. **Provide opportunities for students to explore, communicate, and understand their feelings.** Set aside time for journaling. Student/teacher journaling can be a great way to build rapport and express feelings. Student-to-student journaling is one way to form or strengthen friendships and solve problems. If students are comfortable, suggest they use a parent/child journal at home. Poetry, art, and music are additional ways for students to express their feelings.

92. **Extend students' learning community through the Internet.**
Connect to your students' world. Take them into virtual learning
places by using the Internet in your lessons. Studies have shown
that online literature discussions provide numerous benefits – to
include higher-level thinking skill development. Work with your
fellow teachers to develop a list of viable learning sites. Check
them out first before using them with students. Are they age-
appropriate? They might be an exciting option for the students
who are reading way above their grade level.

93. **Minimize or eliminate disengagement by including everyone
in discussions.** Write each student's name on a separate
popsicle stick or a tongue depressor. Place the sticks in a jar.
Select a different stick each time you solicit a response during
discussions. When all have been set aside, you'll know you
have included everyone.

94. **Share class progress frequently with your students so they
can realize improvement as a team.** Say something like, "I've
noticed fewer spelling mistakes in everyone's writing. Your efforts
are really paying off." Or "I've noticed how quickly you're solving
math problems. That shows how hard you've worked at learning
the basic multiplication facts. Keep it up!"

Additionally, here are some ways to enhance communication between the home and school …

(Note: Throughout this book, the term "parents" is used generically in reference to dual parents, single parents, and guardians.)

95. **Keep parents informed.** Create a Classroom News Blog or a traditional newsletter. Check out a few blog providers such as edublogs.org or blogspot.com. Review your district's "Acceptable Use Policy." Write the blog and inform parents of its existence. Ask for feedback on usefulness of the information. Over time – and depending on your grade level – you might be able to turn over this task to students.

96. **Share good news with parents.** All parents love to hear good things about their children! This can be shared by a phone call, note, or e-mail. Give specific examples of events, achievements, or behaviors that are worth praising.

97. **Conduct periodic parent-teacher conferences.** Agree upon a convenient time for the parents and use the time wisely. Start with a compliment. Share progress. Speak clearly and avoid using educational terms that may impede understanding. Discuss any areas for improvement – along with ways the parents might become involved in their child's learning. Have a follow-up plan … and follow up!

98. **Offer a midyear "How Are Things Going?" meeting for parents.** By the middle of the school year, many things need to be readdressed or updated. Send home a questionnaire asking parents if they need a review of classroom expectations and events. It may be that your newsletters are providing sufficient information.

99. **Give parents a "heads-up call" when necessary.** When you see a decline in a student's work, take five minutes to talk to the student, five minutes to call the parents, and another ten minutes to talk to both so they can address the issue before final grades come out. Discuss specific ways the student can improve – and what the parents might do to help.

100. **Respond to all parent messages.** Voicemails, e-mails, and written notes from parents can be very time-consuming. It is important to respond to all, but at the same time, let it be known that you are not on call 24/7. This can be achieved through a voicemail (or e-mail auto response) that says, "Between the hours of _____ a.m. and _____p.m., I am focused on teaching and attending to the needs of my students. However, your message is important to me, so I will get back to you as soon as possible. If you need my immediate attention, please call the school office at _____ and the secretary will reach me. Thank you for your understanding."

101. **Extend extra effort for language barriers.** Sometimes parents have limited English proficiency. Listen more carefully. Ask when you don't understand. You might say, "I'm sorry; could you please repeat that?" Acknowledge when you do understand what is said. If necessary (and available), involve someone who can translate for you.

102. **Delegate, delegate, delegate!** So many teacher tasks involve communication. Whenever possible (and practical), assign written communication activities to parent volunteers and students. Be sure to check for accuracy of information, punctuation, grammar, and spelling before sending their work out to others.

Reflections on Teaching & Learning

I like a teacher who gives you something to take home to think about besides homework.

~ Lily Tomlin as *Edith Ann*

The mediocre teacher tells.
The good teacher explains.
The superior teacher demonstrates.
The great teacher inspires.

~ William Arthur Ward

If kids come to us [teachers] from strong, healthy, functioning families, it makes our job easier.
If they do not come to us from strong, healthy, functioning families, it makes our job more important.

~ Barbara Colorose

Teachers, I believe, are the most responsible and important members of society because their professional efforts affect the fate of the earth.

~ Helen Caldicott

Chapter 4

It's All About People!

Reaching Out to Others ... and Yourself

I'll never forget the comment a student's dad made to me one June afternoon when I asked to have a conference with him: "Wow, you must really care about my boy. Most teachers would not bother on the last day of school." Even though there had been several previous conferences, it took all year for that dad to conclude that I really DID care about his boy ... that I really was concerned about meeting their needs.

That conversation was one of many reminders for me that: a) teaching is a very complex people puzzle that involves relationships with many others who impact our professional lives, and b) we must handle these relationships with the same levels of attention, effort, and concern that we devote to our lesson plans and classroom activities.

Once we accept that teaching is a multifaceted people business, our next (and BIG) task is to figure out how to make it all run smoothly – for the sake of our students and our own mental health. Keeping in mind that everyone has needs, perceptions, and something to offer, we must reach out, reach out, REACH OUT! Why? Because it matters – not only as educators, but also as caring human beings!

There are some important things to consider when working with those who surround our profession. Most of these tips involve using the same people skills that we teach our students: communication, problem solving, team building, cooperation, collaboration, and many more.

As you read the ideas that follow, think about how putting them into practice could enhance your teaching environment – making it a place you LOVE to return to each day!

Recognizing the importance of our closest stakeholders' needs and concerns, this chapter is divided into several sections: students' needs, parents' needs, fellow teachers' needs, administrators' needs, and your own needs. Based on readings, conversations, observations, and student feedback, these tips should be helpful when dealing with the "people variable" of our profession.

Paying Attention to Students' Needs

A few years ago, I asked a group of former students what they believe are the most important qualities of an effective teacher. Their answers were quite revealing. They felt that teachers needed to know their subjects, have positive attitudes, be interesting, listen well, and be fair, fun, helpful, creative, kind, understanding, and caring. As they described their experiences with teachers, I was able to extract some universal needs which are included in the following:

103. **Be respectful.** Every student is deserving of your respect and efforts. Give it to them and it is likely to be returned. Treat everyone with dignity as you communicate – both verbally and nonverbally. Show interest in each class member. Go the extra mile when helping them.

104. **Set guidelines and structure.** Students cannot monitor their own behavior unless the expectations are clear. They need to know what is expected of them. When the guidelines are clear, the enforcement is consistent, and the consequences are fair and reasonable, students are more likely to comply.

105. **Give them the tools to succeed.** Most students want to enjoy success but need you to teach them the skills required to make that possible. Teach them effective learning strategies that will improve their understanding and performance for each subject. In addition, help them develop effective social, organizational, and study habits. Consider demonstrating the use of graphic information organizers and a variety of test-taking techniques.

106. **Make learning enjoyable.** Through the use of drama, music, humor, physical movement, simulations, and hands-on activities, your students can have fun while learning. (You'll find more suggestions in Chapter 6.)

107. **Keep learning relevant to their world.** Find those learning connections to your students' lives. Through sharing stories of personal experiences along with current events, you may be able to find the hook that will draw their interest. When you include sports, music, movies, hobbies, etc. – in addition to real-life experiences such as field trips – you are more likely to provide relevance for your students.

108. **Expect from students only what you expect of yourself.** For example, I listened to a group of middle school students brutally criticize the dress attire of their teacher. They saw it as a double standard! They couldn't understand the need for their dress code when their teacher didn't follow the same one. Are you meeting your deadlines, producing quality work, dressing and acting appropriately? Remember that YOU are the standard. Students are constantly watching you – and they rightfully assume that it's okay to follow your lead.

109. **Adopt and implement as many of the ideas in this book as possible.** Becoming the most effective teacher you can be is the very best way to meet your students' needs.

Being Attentive to Parents' Needs

Parents have needs, too – one being to hear good things about their children. Who wouldn't want that? In conversations with parents, be sure you talk about specifics related to their child that demonstrate you really know and value that student.

Here are some additional tips that will address what parents need from teachers and administrators:

110. **Try to accommodate parental requests.** If a parent requests special seating, health considerations, or learning accommodations for their child, do your best to make it happen. Remember, parents generally know their child and his or her needs better than anyone else.

111. **Recognize and appreciate their child's uniqueness.** Each student has his/her unique blend of personality, abilities, talents, skills, and interests. Appeal to them by bringing in artifacts, news clips, and books; sharing stories and experiences; and attending events that are important to your students.

112. **Do not judge their child or their family.** Drop all biases and preconceptions of students. Give each student and parent the same respect and attention no matter what the family circumstances may be. Remember that as a teacher your job is to judge academic performance, not people.

113. **Have appropriate expectations for their child.** One size does not fit all. You may need to differentiate instruction. Whether the student requires additional help or challenges, find time and ways to provide it.

114. **Make sure their child starts with a clean slate.** Avoid labels. Student reputations often follow them as they enter new classrooms. Keeping in mind that students respond differently to different teachers and teaching styles, give each student a fresh start when they enter your classroom.

115. **Make parents "partners" in education.** Involve them in interactive homework activities so they know what their children are learning in class. This includes reading, spelling, science experiments, or playing math games together. Offer opportunities to volunteer for those who want to be more involved.

Meeting the Needs of Your Fellow Teachers

- ✓ Give each other the benefit of the doubt.
- ✓ Contribute to each other's success.
- ✓ Share ideas and resources.
- ✓ Celebrate achievements. Give praise and compliments.
- ✓ Respect each other's opinions.
- ✓ Ask for and give help when needed.
- ✓ Be warm and welcoming to new/transferring colleagues.
- ✓ Share the load.
- ✓ Care about each other's wellness.
- ✓ Speak highly of each other.
- ✓ Speak directly to each other when conflicts arise.
- ✓ Do not compete – it's not a popularity contest!
- ✓ Work together as a team.

What Administrators Need From Teachers
(and vice versa)

Successful performance

Understanding

Personal concern, sensitivity

Professionalism

Outstanding leadership

Respect for each other

Teamwork and collaboration

Support for each other is one of the most important gifts teachers and principals can give. Without it, you may as well have an empty principal's office.

Support doesn't mean you have to agree with each other on every issue. It's perfectly reasonable to agree to disagree – yet support each other's role. Support is about being there for each other when it truly matters – when a parent starts ranting or a student throws a tantrum. It means not selling each other out during those tough times. Support includes believing what you see, hear, and experience yourself – not what the gossip chain tells you. It means giving each other the benefit of the doubt and assuming that the other person is well intentioned.

Mutual support does not require establishing a close friendship. Rather, it involves maintaining a healthy working relationship of trust and respect – important components of the school climate.

Attending to Yourself

It was a lousy experience in my life.

I was a relatively young woman with a fifteen-month old baby girl, a seven-year old son, and a very helpful husband. By all accounts, I was pretty healthy until I woke up one morning thinking I would be getting ready for my usual teaching day. Wrong! I didn't know what it was, but I couldn't lift my head off of the pillow. Too weak to drive, a friend took me to a clinic where a chest x-ray confirmed that I had pneumonia – an illness that kept me home from work for two weeks.

I couldn't do a thing but sleep and remain horizontal. I had no clue how this illness would affect my emotional as well as my physical being. The sicker I became, the more I wanted to be in my classroom resuming my normal teaching responsibilities. I wanted to be a mom and wife again. When I didn't bounce back to normal as quickly as I expected, my mind started to go to those "what if" places. The longer my recovery took, the more saddened and concerned I became.

It was that experience which helped me realize how connected my *physical* health was to my *mental* health. It demonstrated to me how vital my wellness was to my daily performance as a mother, a wife, and a teacher.

Since we typically perform at our best when we are healthy and strong, it's imperative that we take care of ourselves. Clearly, our personal wellness affects those around us as well as ourselves. With that in mind, here are some tips that support your physical and emotional health …

116. **Join a social group that meets in person.** Many of us stay connected through popular online social networks. But face-to-face time is equally (if not more) important. Meeting in person provides the opportunity to see, hear, and touch others in ways that computers don't offer: a smile, a hug, eye contact, a nod, laughter, a soothing tone – all signs of genuine warmth you can see, hear, and feel good about.

117. **Do not isolate yourself at work.** Schedule time to chat with colleagues in person instead of e-mailing. Attend colleague social gatherings. Eat lunch with coworkers a few times a week. Such socialization provides a sense of acceptance and belonging which is important to your mental health.

118. **Increase your health consciousness.** This can be hard to follow but important advice nevertheless: Choose foods carefully and exercise regularly. Know your body's signs of illness and see your doctor as needed and for periodic "checkups." Keep your energy levels balanced. Sleep, physical movement, foods, relaxation, and laughter are all contributing factors to that all-important balance.

119. **Explore your interests.** Discover your passions. Find a hobby and fit it into your weekly schedule at home or school. And share it with your students. I used to teach my class members how to macramé – an art that boys and girls enjoyed equally. It was a great inclement weather activity and a source of relaxation and pleasure for me!

120. **Tackle your tension.** Yoga, pilates, music, and massages are good ways to relax. Some additional ways are walks and bike rides. Discover what works for you and do it as often as you can.

121. **Address conflicts, resolve issues.** Interpersonal conflicts with associates typically increase stress and negatively impact your mental and physical health – as well as your performance. Find a way to discuss your issues with those involved. Share your feelings and concerns candidly (and tactfully). Listen to their side. Ask for the person's help in maintaining a mutually respectful working relationship.

122. **Build new friendships, nurture the existing ones.** Take the initiative in arranging a get-together or in organizing or hosting a social event, or just be the first to send an e-mail. You'll be glad you did! Friendships make us richer people.

123. **Perform acts of kindness.** There are many daily opportunities to do kind things for people. Offer to cover a colleague's recess duty when he or she is not feeling well. Share a learning exercise that has worked for you. Help someone carry boxes in from the parking lot. Tell a student how nice he or she looks that day. Such acts will have a positive effect on the other person ... and on you.

124. **Smile, laugh, enjoy your life.** Have you ever walked down the hallway, passing other adults who never say a word? Be the first to smile at them! Surround yourself with fun, upbeat people. Plan fun activities at least once a week – lunch, a movie, a sport, or any other enjoyable activity or event. *Choose* to be positive and enjoy whatever you're doing at any given moment.

125. **Focus on your daily successes.** Reflect on positive things that happen each day. A student's improvement, great behaviors, completed report cards, or making it through a tough lesson are just a few examples of the many reasons you may have to smile and feel good.

126. **Reflect and adjust for continuous improvement.** With few exceptions, all of us share the desire to be the best we can be. Once we see what needs improving, we can begin to make the changes needed to enhance our performance. Dancers practice in rooms lined with mirrors to observe their routines; singers listen through headsets to make sure they're in tune. Take a lesson from them by making videos of your classroom sessions. Review and evaluate your teaching style, body language, verbal communication, interactions with students, etc. Ask for feedback. Set goals for performance improvement and work diligently on them.

127. **Recharge, Renew, Revitalize!** There may be some days when you feel like you're in a slump. That's perfectly normal. In those cases, *recharge* by adding fun activities to your lesson plans (see Chapter 6). *Renew* by changing your classroom environment (room arrangement, décor, seating, etc.). *Revitalize* by walking for 20 minutes with a few of your colleagues or students.

128. **Notice and appreciate the simple things in your life.** Pay close attention to the world around you. Its beauty will bring a new perspective to your day. Use all of your senses to focus on the trees, flowers, birds, raindrops, lakes, and all other gifts of nature. Be thankful for everything.

> *People who live the most fulfilling lives are the ones who are always rejoicing at what they have.*
> ~ Richard Carlson

129. **Have hopes, dreams, and goals for your future.** This helps you stay positive, which is important to your mental health. Take a moment and reflect upon what's really important to you. Anytime is a good time to build your "bucket list." Include all of the things you'd like to do and places you'd like to see before leaving this earth. Start doing them!

130. **Believe in yourself! Develop confidence.** Collect the artifacts of your successful teaching moments. Chances are there are many more than you may think. Start building a scrapbook with positive notes from parents and students. Include photos of fun times with your students, awards, certificates, class transcripts, etc. Look through it often to remind yourself about your many accomplishments and the great job you're doing!

131. **Create more "feel good" moments.** Praise the people who make your days more manageable through their efficiency, kindness, and willingness to help. The custodian, the school secretary, lunchroom staff, playground supervisors, instructional aides, and other support staff all play an important role in your day. Don't take them for granted. Be sure to tell them and their boss about their special performance. Teach your students to do the same.

132. **Balance your life.** Prioritize and focus on what's most important to you. Family, friends, and job may be your priorities, but do you give each their fair share of your time? If your time allocations are lopsided, adjust. Know when to put your work aside.

133. **Avoid overextending yourself.** Gracefully decline requests for additional work when your "plate" is full. Simply say, "I'd love to help you out, but I'm having difficulty getting my own work completed right now. Maybe in a few days." Doing so demonstrates a desire to be helpful – and a willingness to be of assistance in the future when things ease up.

More *Reflections*
on Teaching & Learning

A good teacher is one who can understand those who are not very good at explaining, and explain to those who are not very good at understanding.

~ Dwight D. Eisenhower

Education is not the filling of a pail, but the lighting of a fire.

~ William Butler Yeats

You learn more quickly under the guidance of experienced teachers. You waste a lot of time going down blind alleys if you have no one to lead you.

~ W. Somerset Maugham

I am a teacher. A teacher is someone who leads. There is no magic here. I do not walk on water; I do not part the sea. I just love children.

~ Marva Collins

Chapter 5

Music, Hoops, and Memory Builders

Creating Those Fun Moments That Enhance Learning

Think back to your early education. Do you remember your favorite teacher? What did he or she do differently that still puts a smile on your face? Chances are that your favorite teacher planned fun-filled activities that made your learning memorable.

Are you looking to recreate those fun, yet meaningful learning moments with your students? It's possible with strategic planning and by keeping several principles in mind. Your responsibility is to present the curriculum in a way that enables the students to make relevant connections to their lives. Expanding the students' prior knowledge, defining the purpose and usefulness of information, and providing fun, yet meaningful learning experiences are some of the ways to increase motivation and relevance. Most students want to know why they have to study certain information or complete a given assignment. They also want to know how they can achieve success. The more you explain and justify the lesson or activity, the greater the likelihood that they will become motivated and engaged in their learning.

In addition to creating the best learning environment, being organized, and communicating successfully, effective teaching means involving students in highly motivating, outcome-based activities that achieve a learning goal. With that in mind, try some of these activities that will enhance learning and leave memorable footprints in the minds of the students you teach ...

134. **Engage students in activities that evoke positive emotions.** Clapping or tapping rhythms, singing and chanting, snapping fingers, and moving the body are just a few ways to stir positive emotions. For example, along with students, snap your fingers for each letter as you spell a word aloud. Snapping, clapping, or tapping can also be applied to basic math facts, historical names, dates and events, and many other learning concepts.

135. **Provide choices.** Choices for learning opportunities can be presented in a variety of ways. Here's one suggestion: Set up learning centers within your classroom for poetry writing, math challenges, art exploration, or music enrichment. Provide time for students to visit the centers of their choice. Require the use of "reflection sheets" for documenting what they accomplished or learned – and for planning goals for their next visit.

136. **Encourage ALL students to assume leadership roles.** Create opportunities for everyone to lead. When you empower students through leadership roles, their undiscovered talents will often rise to the occasion. Offer those roles to the underachievers, the less popular, and those unlikely to assert themselves. Gently nudge them when confidence is lacking. Support and guide them toward success with the help of those who normally "shine."

137. **Challenge and expand student thinking through debates.** Debates encourage divergent responses, allow students to learn from each other, help students develop convincing arguments, and foster respect of others' opinions. Teach the format – and be sure to facilitate/manage the activity. Debate current issues that are relevant to the students' lives or futures.

138. **Provide life-use experiences.** For example, set up a BANK and one or two retail stores in your classroom. Together, plan ways to earn classroom cash (fake money). Included could be peer-tutoring sessions, housekeeping duties, homework helper, etc. Interview and hire employees for your BANK and retail stores. Make and use a simple Job Application Form for applicants to fill out. Conduct interviews and hire students for various positions.

139. **Address career education at every grade level.** Invite community leaders, business owners, and professional parents to speak to your classes about preparing for future employment. Arrange field trips to encourage students to explore a variety of job possibilities. Exposure and additional research will help students acquaint themselves with work options – important information for planning their educational and career goals.

140. **Encourage compassion and collaboration through service work.** Discuss the importance of volunteer work and present various projects that involve group participation – for example, spring cleanup, raking leaves, or assisting elderly citizens with chores and errands. Have the students select one group project. Obtain parental permission. Organize the activity – and involve everyone. In addition to fostering a sense of accomplishment and giving, it will enhance teamwork and collaboration.

141. **Encourage physical health.** Have students and parents plan a Healthy Lifestyles Fair as a fundraiser. All activities should focus on healthy living habits. For example, food booths would offer only nutritional options, and skill games would promote activities that help strengthen the heart and muscles.

142. **Recognize and promote nonacademic talent.** Create opportunities to "perform" as options for recess. Provide a stage for those who would like to share their talents. They may want to act, sing, dance, or play a musical instrument. This can spark their interest in performing arts careers. And other talents – such as athletics, writing, art, photography, etc. – often emerge when students are given the chance to explore a variety of interests.

143. **Build humor and laughter into your daily activities.** The positive benefits of laughter are well documented. It produces useful brain chemicals, reduces stress, and enhances enjoyment. One way to encourage it in your classroom is to have students organize a "Comedy Club." The club members could search for appropriate jokes, humorous quotes, video clips, cartoons, funny songs, etc. that they could post, sing, or play as students enter the classroom in the morning. It starts the day with a smile! This will add interest and enthusiasm to your learning environment, and it will help reinforce what types of humor are appropriate and acceptable – and which are not.

144. **Practice math skills with "hoops"!** Hang a small basketball hoop over your classroom door. Divide your students into two teams. Using a foam basketball, the shooting team scores two points when making a basket from one designated line, and three points from a line farther away. Each student takes three shots. The opposing team creates and solves either multiplication or addition problems from the scores of each shooter.

145. **Incorporate artistic drama.** One example is to have students role-play or dramatize a silly or serious poem or story. They could also do a forensic presentation or write a musical play to reinforce a unit of learning.

146. **Combine writing, music, and learning.** As a group, compose a song that could be used to reinforce learning concepts. This could include a math rap, a history or geography song, or any other concept-laden lyrics that could be sung to a familiar tune. Students will remember the song and concepts for many years to come. Don't you remember the ABC song?

147. **Use students to teach social skills.** For example, if you want to reduce bullying or increase respect at your school, recruit a group of volunteer students to write and deliver a script and/or skit that sends the desired message about interacting respectfully. Help them rehearse for a presentation at a school assembly.

> *Tell me and I forget. Teach me and I remember.*
> *Involve me and I learn.*
>
> ~ Benjamin Franklin
> *(similar quotation attributed to Confucius)*

148. **Keep students informed about appropriate local, national, and world news.** Have your students start a "Current Events" scrapbook (on paper or electronically). Each student selects a news article that captures his or her interest, reads the article, briefly summarizes it, and writes a reaction – all of which are shared with the class. While this weekly activity offers a wide range of learning opportunities, it also gives students a more global perspective beyond their own world.

149. **Popcorn, Popsicles, and Poetry.** Have your class write poems about ordinary experiences and/or objects. For example, on a hot day, pass out popsicles for students to observe and describe (and eat). How do these slowly melting treats look, taste, and feel as students lick them? Encourage using a variety of poem types (after previously teaching them) – including acrostic and haiku. Next time, in smaller groups, repeat the writing experience with popcorn seeds. Heat them (or air pop) and have students observe the popping – and describe the sound, appearance, feel, and taste.

150. **Create useful, meaningful, homework assignments.** Not all homework needs to be skill textbook driven. For example, as a math assignment students could check the accuracy of a grocery store receipt. Other useful assignments could include a shopping trip to the grocery store to compare prices or nutritional information, cooking a meal following a recipe with measurements, or similar activities that involve life-learning skills.

151. **Plan a "high interest" afternoon once a month for curriculum-related activities.** Use parent volunteers or invite guests who will set up and conduct mini-workshops. For example, if studying about Japan, one guest could demonstrate preparing, cooking, and serving a few Japanese food dishes; another could teach simple origami or how to write a haiku poem. Your end-of-year celebration could be a culmination of learned concepts by offering a wider variety of workshops throughout the entire day.

152. **Extend your thoughtfulness and generosity** by giving those memorable, extra special touches. When I taught a continuing education class for teachers, I welcomed them by placing a fresh flower on each of their desks. You could welcome your entering class with a fortune cookie containing a special message, a tiny bag of fruit candy, or a coupon for a special privilege. Be creative.

153. **Build uniqueness by "branding" yourselves.** Give your class a positive group personality. Design a classroom logo. Create a motto. Together write a song about the positives of your group. Use the logo on group products, posters, T-shirts, etc. Wear the T-shirts when going on field trips and attending assemblies.

154. **Reward your class for group efforts.** Encourage group as well as individual accountability. Fill a bowl with three different-colored marbles – each color representing a certain number of points. Together, agree on three weekly group goals. Assign each goal the color of a marble (e.g., good manners = red, etc.) Each time a group goal is earned, have a student place a marble in a cup or jar. Total up the points at the end of each half-day. Give a special privilege for the maximum points earned at the end of each day.

155. **Strengthen team building** while reinforcing academic and social skills such as decision making, reading and following directions, cooperation, leadership, etc. Organize curriculum-related scavenger hunts. Form teams and give each a list of words, numbers, etc. to search for. Turn them loose as they look for the items on their list. The first team to complete the list wins!

156. **Inspire creativity and initiative by doing the following:**

- Provide opportunities to explore and create.
- Believe in the student's potential.
- Allow students to decide on approaches to assignments.
- Trust their decisions and plans.
- Give students permission to take risks.
- Minimize or eliminate the fear of making mistakes.
- Encourage students to think "out of the box."

157. **Use games for brain challenges.** For example, mimic familiar television quiz shows that challenge contestants on their knowledge of a variety of subjects. Substitute questions that relate to your curriculum. Include music and sound effects (e.g., ticking clock) to enhance the experience.

158. **Get "out of the box" yourself!** Spark your students' interest with props, gimmicks, costumes, and any other novelty ideas that capture their interest and pique their curiosity. Occasionally, act silly – kids love it! *When you entertain, your students retain.*

159. **Eliminate the boredom of routine.** Change the color of your handouts each week. Use different ink colors for correcting. Let students select the color. Change what you are doing frequently. Include periodic "turn and talks" for discussion. Allow students to take stretching breaks. Present riddles or trivia during breaks. Change the look and layout of your classroom periodically.

160. **Use technology as much as possible.** Research, projects, creative work, written communication, etc., can all be enhanced through technology. Help students learn and use the Internet, PowerPoint®, digital video and a variety of available software that can enhance assignments and presentations. And be sure to use them in the delivery of *your* lessons.

161. **Help them learn while stretching their imaginations.** Here's a creative activity that involves everyone in developing a story, strengthens listening skills, and focuses on the use of adjectives: Everyone starts by standing. The teacher begins with a starter sentence, "One dark, cold October night ..." and tosses a foam ball to a student who completes the sentence by adding his/her ideas. That student tosses the ball to someone else and sits down. The process continues until the last student brings the story to an end.

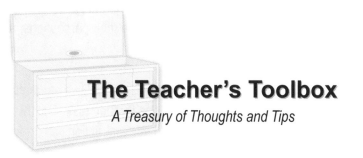

Chapter 6

The Teacher's Toolbox

A Treasury of Thoughts and Tips

As educators and lifelong learners, we know that becoming a more effective teacher is an ongoing journey of practice, reflections, and adjustments. Each of us comes equipped with a virtual *Teacher's Toolbox,* and we improve our skills by filling that box with ideas, tips, strategies, and techniques from each other.

We acquire teaching "tools" from many sources, but rarely do we have the opportunity to collect and share ideas from across the country and beyond. Well, we have done that for you by soliciting ideas from literally thousands of walkthetalk.com users, worldwide. Their input has been used throughout this work and provides the content for this final chapter.

We invite you to fill *your* toolbox with some of the treasures from our potpourri of useful thoughts about effective teaching. Because of the overwhelming number of submissions, we were able to include only a small portion of the ideas received. Nevertheless, we're confident that you'll find the following pages very thought-provoking. We encourage you to take this wisdom and absorb, adapt, and apply it to your special situation.

> ## I am still learning.
> ~ Michelangelo

162. **Look through your students' "window of perception."** Listen to understand how your students think, feel, and perceive. Try to see things as they do. Imagine and realize their perceptions. Ask about them for a clearer understanding.

163. **Don't talk too much!** Sometimes less is more. Give students an introduction and necessary instructions for their task. Get them started on the activity. Fine-tune and add instructions as needed.

164. **Bridge the gap.** Make connections with students by building trust, giving attention, and creating open dialogues to fill the void in many of their lives. Be a trusted adult and proper influence that they may need to become responsible citizens.

165. **Raise the curiosity of students** so they are eager to investigate. You can do this through demonstrations, challenging questions, stories, civic issues and/or problems, and real-life dilemmas.

166. **Impart resiliency skills so students can rise above adversity.** Here's the inspiring comment from a teacher to a now-respected, successful author, actor, and speaker who rose above poverty and illiteracy in India: "When I was born, I was an ordinary person because it was just beyond my control, but when I will die, I will certainly die as an extraordinary person because it is definitely in my control." Often it's the words – and especially the example – of a teacher that inspires resiliency.

167. **Extend appropriate affection by offering students one of the 3 H's: a Handshake, a Hi-5, or a Hug!** Your offer of affection may be the only one that student receives that day. The warmth of <u>appropriate</u> touching is a sign of the approval, acceptance, and trust so greatly needed by all!

168. **Give SPECIAL praise for a SPECIAL reason.** It might sound like this: I loved the last essay you wrote! I'm so proud of your writing talent! You are truly a gifted writer who I believe will be very successful one day.

169. **Ask for and welcome student feedback.** Find out how your students think you're doing as a teacher. Create a questionnaire. Make student comment cards with questions and a rating scale. Leave space for comments or suggestions. Use them often.

170. **Notice and attend to the quiet students, too!** Quiet, average students often get lost in the crowd simply because others require more time and attention. Draw them into your discussions. Help build confidence by praising their comments. Offer opportunities for them to be involved and noticed. Select them for leadership roles, as helpers, or simply offer frequent encouraging words.

171. **Foster independence.** Allow students, regardless of age, every opportunity to carry out tasks on their own. Picking up paper, clearing tables, putting away resources, etc., are chores that encourage them to become responsible, independent individuals.

172. **Monitor progress.** Do a short, simple, basic baseline for all subjects – targeting skills like fluency, comprehension, organization of written thoughts, spelling, multiplication facts, etc. Midyear, do another sample with the same test and directions. Analyze each student's progress and share with students and parents.

173. **Close with reflection.** End each day in a meaningful, calm way by providing time for students to discuss and think about their academic and social learning. Ask questions such as: "What one thing did you learn in science today? What made you happy or sad during recess today? What would you like to spend more time on tomorrow?"

174. **Be a passionate learner!** Learn from your students. Refresh your skills by attending workshops, conferences, and classes and by reading educational materials. Form learning groups. Have discussions with those who challenge your viewpoints. You will benefit ... and so will your students!

175. **Accommodate needs by recording a video of your lessons.** There are many benefits to having a record of your lessons. Students with special needs can review the lessons for better understanding. Absentees are able to catch up by viewing what they missed. All students can use the videos to review concepts and reinforce learning.

176. **Remember the 4 C's:** Communication, Clutter-free, Community outreach, Classroom management! All are important habits to develop. The art of teaching is a work in progress. Don't try to be everything and do everything all at once.

177. **Polish those gems!** Teaching and guiding students is like polishing diamonds. Teachers often detect a hidden sparkle in a student. Being able to distinguish, recognize, and polish those hidden gems is a unique gift found in extraordinary teachers. Teachers shape destinies by applying loving pressure to what some see as only a lump of coal. Never underestimate the power of applying steady encouragement to develop hidden brilliance.

178. **Give extra help whenever needed.** Before, during, and after school are all times to hang your "help available" sign out.

179. **Be analytical and results oriented.** Do more than administer and correct tests. Observe student test-taking behaviors. Is the student easily distracted, tired, guessing at answers? Do you need to make testing modifications? Analyze test results. Look for patterns of errors. Re-teach when necessary.

180. Use "The ABC's of an A+ Teacher" as your guide to becoming the best teacher, employee, and person you can be:

Aa Accountable and Accessible

Bb Bright and Believable

Cc Caring and Consistent

Dd Devoted and Diplomatic

Ee Empathetic and Engaging

Ff Friendly and Focused

Gg Genuine and Guiding

Hh Humorous and Helpful

Ii Inviting and Imaginative

Jj Judicious and Joyful

Kk Kind and Knowledgeable

Ll Listening and Loyal

Mm Motivating and Memorable

Nn Nonjudgmental and Nurturing

Oo Open-hearted and Open-minded

Pp Patient and Passionate

Qq	**Q**uizzical and **Q**uality-oriented
Rr	**R**espectful and **R**eliable
Ss	**S**ensitive and **S**ensible
Tt	**T**rustworthy and **T**actful
Uu	**U**nderstanding and **U**plifting
Vv	**V**ersatile and **V**igilant
Ww	**W**ise and **W**arm
X	**X**tra effort-giving
Y	**Y**oung at heart
Z	**Z**ealous

CLOSING THOUGHTS

Obviously, our common role as educators is to facilitate successful learning. But we also share a deeper purpose that goes far beyond the mere transference of knowledge and imparting of the classical 3 R's. That purpose is to guide and develop productive members of society – individuals who are socially competent, eager and willing to learn and who seek out new information, critique it, apply it, and share it with others. Ultimately, we are here to help develop informed citizens capable of functioning as contributors to a complex and ever-changing global environment.

THAT is the *essence* of education … that is what truly effective teaching is all about!

You know, it's been said that "it takes a village to raise a child." Well, I disagree. I believe it takes a loving, caring, involved *family* to raise a child. It does, however, take a "village" to **educate** a child.

All of us who work within schools and school districts are crucial members of each student's "village." Our collective responsibility is to teach, support, encourage, praise, and enhance their knowledge, efforts, and achievements. And, we are here to assist the families of our students in meeting *their* responsibilities as well. In doing so, each of us makes a difference in the lives of students in our own special way.

Now, more than ever, we "villagers" need to come together, combine our efforts, and empower our students to become the citizens of the future who will lead our society as problem-solvers and peacekeepers. We need to be the most effective at what we do so that our students can do the same. The book has provided a handful of suggestions and tips to help you make that happen.

As a fellow lifelong learner, I'm confident that you will continue to practice the best teaching methods and strategies available. When all else fails, trust your instincts and do what you feel is right for the kids who depend so greatly upon you. There will be challenges, but stay on the path – it's well worth the journey!

I am blessed to share in your professional calling. And like you, I am honored to proudly state …

I AM a teacher!

Louise Paris

I touch the future.
I TEACH.

~ Christa McAuliffe

CONTENT CONTRIBUTORS

A grateful acknowledgment and sincere thank you to the following educators, parents, and students for contributing ideas which were used periodically throughout this work:

LaNelle Agee, Odessa, TX   **Boleyn Andrist,** Eyota, MN

Sastry Asn, Andhrapradesh, India

Kaitlyn Viva Balson, Airdrie, Alberta, Canada

Lauren Moulton-Beaudry, Ed.D., Pasadena, CA

Wayne Bell, Fair Oaks, CA   **Maryellen Berry,** Marietta, GA

Carol Bone, Gold River, CA   **Ann Bonner,** Baltimore, MD

Catherine S. Browers, Big Rapids, MI

Cathy Brown, Edmonton, Alberta, Canada

Ron Brown, Laguna Hills, CA   **Carmen Buchanan,** Madison, AL

Nancy Casey, Hudson, FL   **Jackie Reese Clark,** Murdock, MN

Joseph D. Compton, Wichita, KS   **Kathryn Cook,** Sugar Land, TX

Dora Daniluk, Katy, TX   **Dennis Docheff,** Warrensburg, MO

Dr. Craig Domeck, Orlando, FL   **Melissa Drake,** Fort Myers, FL

Mary Dziczkowski, Medina, OH   **Clarissa Evans,** Orlando, FL

Marsha C. Fearrington, Graham, NC   **Carla Jean Foster,** San Diego, CA

Jim Gentil, Austin, TX   **Victoria Gerow,** Brecksville, OH

Filomena Giannico, Norwalk, CT   **Karen Giesler,** Kirkwood, MO

Carol Giomuso, Cleveland, OH   **Amber Gregg,** Sioux City, IA

Annie Hansen, Westtown, NY   **Nancy Harvey,** Flower Mound, TX

Melody Hassell, Talisheek, LA   **Rich Hebbel,** Davenport, LA

Wendy Herring, Wilmington, NC   **Fritz Hollenbach,** Beloit, WI

Russell M. Honeycutt, Whiteville, NC

Danelle Hueging, Winnipeg, Manitoba, Canada   **Davi Ingram,** Tyler, TX

Suzanne Jamieson, Wellington, New Zealand

Diane Johnston, Edmonds, WA

Lynne Hope-Jones, London, Ontario, Canada

Karen Keffeler, Plymouth, MN   Cheryl Khera, Bellevue, WA

Julaine R. Kiehn, Columbia, MO   Gerald Kovarik, Northbrook, IL

Suzie Lak, Clearwater, FL   Landa Leavy, West Hartland, CT

Tanya Levy, Port Hawkesbury, Nova Scotia   Miriam Lia, Kalkara, Malta

Jeff Little, Newnan, GA   Oneida Lopez, Philadelphia, PA

Marion, Norseman, Western Australia

Timothy J. Martino, Sterling, VA   Joan Maywalt, Oswego, NY

Rosemary McCloskey, Belfast, Northern Ireland

Steve McLean, Stittsville, Ontario, Canada

Linda McRae, Cloverdale, British Columbia, Canada

Judith Miner, Nixa, MO   Krista Montgomery, Westernport, MD

Mark Moss, Aliso Viejo, CA   Jhoanna Mukai, Lakeland, FL

Barbie M. Muller, Coeur d'Alene, ID

Zenaida Sanchez Naga, Marawi City, Lanao del Sur, Philippines

Ginny Nance, New Braunfels, TX   Julie Oliver, Sevierville, TN

Susan Paul, Houston, TX   Denise Pistana, Highland, MI

Christopher Pollak, Sayville, NY   Emily Porter, Herington, KS

Kunal Pujara, Evanston, IL   Stephen R. Roberts, Washington, DC

Robert P. Roden, North Canton, OH   Megan Romano, New Britain, PA

Erika Ruiz, Doral, FL   Lisa Schilling, Trenton, MO

Steve Schultz, Fountain Valley, CA   Theresa Shirley, Sparks, NV

Angie Shockley, Davis, WV   Ginger Smith, Nashville, TN

Jacqueline A. Smith, Miami, FL

Keitha Story-Stephenson, Ph.D., Paradise, TX

David Stepp, Kansas City, MO   Cynthia Stotlar, Topeka, KS

Arleen Stroud, Dayton, TX   Diane Thomason, Coralville, IA

Kathy Toenjes, Lakeville, MN   Marie Toole, Delray Beach, FL

Norma E. Van Horn, Cathedral City, CA   Amy Wagoner, Hutchinson, KS

Erika Westmoreland, Highland Village, TX   Gary Williams, St. Augustine, FL

Maruti Yadav, Pune, Maharashtra, India

Renee Zimmerman, Baraboo, WI   Babs Zurcher, Mesa, AZ

THE AUTHOR

Louise Paris

During her thirty-four years as a second and third grade classroom teacher, Louise assumed many leadership roles including committee chairs; AODA facilitator; organizer of peer mediation programs; grant cowriter; curriculum developer for career education, guidance, and gifted education; developer and organizer of Senior Citizens Day; and producer of several musical programs.

Since leaving the classroom, she has continued her work in education through her workshops, classes, and volunteer work for organizations that promote literacy.

Louise designs, makes, and markets a product line of gifts that promote adult/child interaction and literacy. With a passion for writing, she has also authored a wide range of poems.

She can be contacted at **louisemparis@yahoo.com**

THE PUBLISHER

For over 30 years, WalkTheTalk.com has been dedicated to one simple goal...one single mission: *To provide you and your organization with high-impact resources for your personal and professional success.*

Walk The Talk resources are designed to:

- Develop your skills and confidence

- Inspire your team

- Create customer enthusiasm

- Build leadership skills

- Stretch your mind

- Handle tough "people problems"

- Develop a culture of respect and responsibility

- And, most importantly, help you achieve your personal and professional goals.

Contact the Walk The Talk team at
1.888.822.9255
or visit us at www.walkthetalk.com

WALKTHETALK.COM

Resources for Personal and Professional Success

A+ TEACHING

180 Ways to Enhance Your Success as a Teacher

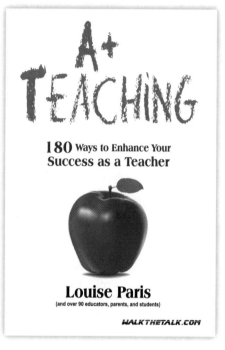

Available in 2 formats!

Softcover Book – $12.95   **Digital Format (eBook) – $8.95**

You play a critically important role. You, along with every other member of your profession, have earned the honor and privilege of proudly proclaiming:

"I AM A TEACHER!"

This is the book you will want your entire education staff reading and using TODAY!

Help yourself and your colleagues achieve even greater levels of teaching effectiveness with the

Personal and Professional Success Kit

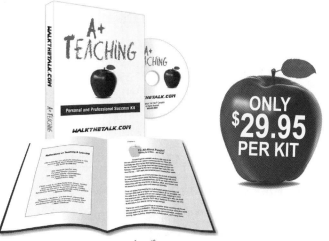

This "must-have" DVD companion to the A+ TEACHING book includes:

- A powerful 3-minute movie tribute to teachers which recognizes their critically important roles and encourages them to always be the best they can be.
Great meeting starter and in-service training supplement!

- Individual learning exercises and action planner to enhance your personal effectiveness and success as a teacher.
Practical self-development tools – just for you!

- Group discussion questions and learning exercises that encourage everyone on your teaching team to apply the tips, strategies, and principles presented in A+ TEACHING.
Perfect for staff meetings and in-service sessions!

Order A+ TEACHING Resources at
www.walkthetalk.com or call 888.822.9255

Visit

WALKTHETALK.COM

Resources for Personal and Professional Success

to learn more about our:

Leadership & Personal Development Center

- Develop leadership skills
- Motivate your team
- Achieve business results

Greenhouse Bookstore

- Save time
- Save money
- Save the planet

Free Newsletters

- The Leadership Solution
- New Products and Special Offers
- New Arrivals in the Greenhouse Bookstore

Motivational Gift Books

- Inspire your team
- Create customer enthusiasm
- Reinforce core values